WAYS OF THE
HEART
GAINING STRENGTH
ALONG THE WAY

A Collection of Poetry and Short Stories

KEVIN J. STE. MARIE

authorHOUSE®

AuthorHouse™
1663 Liberty Drive
Bloomington, IN 47403
www.authorhouse.com
Phone: 1 (800) 839-8640

Published by AuthorHouse 06/15/2018

ISBN: 978-1-5462-4251-2 (sc)
ISBN: 978-1-5462-4249-9 (hc)
ISBN: 978-1-5462-4250-5 (e)

Library of Congress Control Number: 2018906018

Print information available on the last page.

About the Book

This collection of poetry and short stories is all about never leaving anything on the shelf. As a child, I was always curious, and when I learned of my adoption at the age of eight, it changed me. I internally knew I was different but have always been thankful for my mother's love. I believe that it was one of the things that kept me alive when I was lucky enough to be her son. I always enjoyed writing my feelings. I always thought it was the expression of emotion that proves the passion we hold.

I also never thought it should be bottled up. I remember writing these works in some of the most uncertain and hurtful times of my life.

Through the years I have had very intense dreams. I've had many as a young adult and have continued to grow more vivid through the years. Some of these dreams and states have felt like deep memories of things I have seen from other timelines.

As I would write these thoughts and memories, it was like metaphorically dusting traumas from the shelves of life. Through the years, many have read these works and have shared that some of the stories and words have helped them with their challenges. So I set it as a goal to continue to write more until I reached the age of forty. At this time, I would publish it despite criticism or judgment.

I hope that anyone who can take something positive from this collection can see that life is worth living. I also thank you for allowing this book to become a part of your thoughts.

Contents

Chapter 1

STRENGTH

To me strength is traveling to view many people and their struggles. Asking them questions and being happy with all of their answers. Having empathy and sending love to those less fortunate of lives that we have lived. The most beautiful lessons are going to be learned when you least expect it. This is what is so beautiful again about life as a whole. One constant reminder of mine to stay strong was the understanding of knowing what I like internally. When you are sentient to what and who you are it takes less time to move forward. It took me a full 36 years of life to actually write down what I truly wanted. After this happened and started to happen on a regular basis I learned my struggles with strength were not as difficult. It's a lesson I wish I would have been more honest with myself about earlier. But I truly had to experience forgiveness beforehand. I wish you amazing strength in your lifetimes. ~ Kevin J. Ste Marie

Appreciate Your Life - For Once

Running out of land
Straight for the water (rocking)
Swaying, comfortably
Comfortably rocking, moving to (GOD)'s own power
No one knowing what can happen,
EVER
Water, stricken by way of the wheel
Always intravenously warm,
Knowing to never be defeated by such a force.
Cold,
A feeling of heat strikes your twirling body
At the point of your last breath.
Close your eyes, remove your senses
Run to your exits, death is near.
Steel,
The way your blood feels, boiling inside
Pumping towards the end,.

The end of your minds sanity,
The sanity that can make you immortal, (bionic)
Indestructible,
Wish to the genie, now, find the lamp,
Wish for your miracle while you finally open your eyes
And open them wider to see me going by you.

You see,
I am bionic, immortal

You should trust me, to prove my theories,
Prove my thoughts,
Because like the child,
You are gasping, gasping for the air that no human gives you.
It is merely a gift you see?
Don't take these gifts for granted
Didn't (they) ever tell you that?

I am in front of you,
And in my mind, I am calm,
Cold from near death, but calm,
But I know your heart is pumping in and out.
Your nervousness,
Is my fuel
I smile, then I swim, again,
Knowing you are trying to catch up to follow my bubbles in the water,
I hold in,
Try and keep up,

If you can, you will live.
And only then will you see through your survival
Your mistakes.

Learn how easy it is to die and never see it coming,
Appreciate your life, appreciate what you have.

For once!

Beauty - Endless

Clearly a point of discussion,
Feverishly a distraction of fate,
Typically a rise of power,
As we all sit and wait,

Running scared on the bridge,
Thoughts scanning the brain,
Being hit, flipping around,
Driving me insane,

Being able to fly,
Spanning globes never seen,
Running again for the mountains,
So I can fly through time,

The brain is your key,
The body is your temple,
The soul is your balance,
Your consumptions are your death.

Drowning is your fate,
To feel your last breath,
And feel a burning flood of water down your throat,

To feel your soul rising high,
As you see your body calmly fading,
Lowered to the ocean floor.
The beauty of no weight,
Endless.

Disgust - Who Knows

Can I dream a new dream?
Can I feel a new feeling?
Will I see a new sight?
Will I feel a new fright?

Can I be your one?
Will I be a lot of fun?
For you,
The one who will use,
To the end,
Until nothing left is there,

I don't know if I can bear,
The pain,
I'm going insane,

Will I ever be the one or am I just a laugh,
Will you ever be the one I will have?

I pace on the ground,
Thinking what could be the love that I found,
Will we be?
Maybe,

Or will we part,

Who knows?

But when I meet you on the street,
And kiss you,
Will you leave from fright?
Or from disgust,

We will see!

Fall In Love - Forever

You know what hurts
Feeling.
Feeling so hard that one day
An unknown occurrence happens,
Something unexplainable,
A natural disaster,
Naturally killing you to the point,
Of never turning your back from your cares.
You finally get there.
You learn what kills you, that one true thing,
Emotionally and physically,
You race with emotion to see her,
And she is with someone,
Someone that does not respect the love you feel,
Someone who is there for lust,
Not love,
Never will they feel.
Never will anyone understand how much you do, feel,
Hopefully, GOD, what is it that you are telling me? AM I going to bump into her?
Let me know; I am wasting time,
Wasting my feelings, wasting all these emotions, for someone,
Someone who I can love.

Where are you, are you in front of me?
Or are you going to drop into my hands?
Please, bump, me, I need it, you do too if you feel the same,

Denial is your victim, don't victimize yourself.
Fall in love, with me, forever!

Freedom Is In The Heart

There are so many reasons to live.

The people you may meet the next day, the people you met the day before to remember and say hello again when the time comes.

There is also time to say hello to you. To feel your mind in a certain place, only you can enter, and leave with a feeling of hope.

A feeling that you will fight to survive with every breath that the world gives you to breathe.

However, sometimes in life, we may feel depression, anger, fright, and pain. These are feelings I know well. Nevertheless, to all this negativity, you must find the center of yourself, that fire that burns so deep that it gives you the strength to open your eyes each morning.

Your first thought, usually your best. Like your first kiss, of course, fright, the feeling of uncontrollable love will come from your fire telling you this kiss you can never take back.

You will never have another.

For some, anger; to never feel firsts such as these. I drop an hour of my life for these people for the strength to know they can live on and survive.

Depression, I have been here so many times. It has brought me the most strength in my life.

The greatest ideas, and biggest difficulties to accomplish.

However, what is important is that I, and I alone conquered my battles. That I can look back on my best days living, and know that I am loved

Know that I have people who care for me

Even when I sometimes do not want to be cared for

Is it something about me? Maybe.

But to my happiness in life, I would give it up to see others who are less fortunate feel how good it is to love themselves.
Finally when your fire is found,
when the courage has entered the mind, can you look off a mountain and breathe in the air knowing what it must feel like to be free.

Free like me!

This is from the deepest pains and smiles of my heart. I hope you too, one day can feel what I do. This is my wish for you.

I Breathe In Happiness

Sometimes, when I'm alone,
I wonder,
And just when I feel I have lost my thought,
The wind blows,
It blows so hard that I smile,
I feel relief.
In a way it's life,
But in my way, it's a pull,
In the right direction
To remind me;
A reminder that there is something I need to do.
Someone I need to meet.
Someone waiting?

In my opinion, I meet many,
Many who have taught me valuable tools?
Valuable tools of life and survival.
But when a new experience arrives so beautiful
My everyday depression and search for what is right leaves.
It leaves me speechless,
Silent, to wait for a new wind.
Hoping that it will whisper something new into my ear,

Something that will change my life as I've never known?

The Whisper: (happiness).

I know I can be trusted,

I know I can be secure, and also faithful.

I, in my heart, would be amazed to know what you think, what concerns you.

Because our problems can bring our similarities to teach us new things.

But most of all,

We will see what it is like to smile,

And to feel the romance of knowing

That for once, instead of wondering where is this perfect person,

We will already know, won't we?

It will only take a look.

...If we are ever alone, ever lonely, ever scared,

We can look into the sky; breathe deeply.

Then start to feel the wind blowing,

You will see your clothes start to move from the force,

Then you will look at others to see their clothes in a still position,

Only you will be able to feel the wind.

And as it gets stronger, you may start to get a chill,

But not a chill from fright,

A chill to know that you are safe,

So when we close our eyes and breathe in this wind,

We will know that we are loved!

Unconditionally.

Forever.

My Particle Heart

I will find where I need to be
I swear it to the Gods
I will find where I belong
I swear it to the angels
I can do anything
I can bring anyone along
I can lead the army into battle
It's just a relic that I am.

Put me on your mantle
But don't let me collect dust

Dust.

Particles of elimination which
Are to me, the kryptonite of my heart,
Neglect of my soul.

Take care of me,
As I will you,
Because only then will we be meant to be!

Poem For Souls

I had a friend; I still do in my heart.
He is with me every day, in my thoughts,
No disagreements, just youth.

I can only remember our memories, the fun,
But sometimes the fun ends,
And memories are all you are left with,
Staring,

Staring deep into your soul, into your dreams
And riding your mind of thoughts which will never be answered,

Was I a good enough friend?
Was I there every moment?
Will we meet again?
Are you with us?
Do you know how much your family loves you?

These questions are what I know,
And wonder, but they are what I see in my heart in every thought
of you.
I know you are where you need to be, this is why I am strong,
This is why we all are and remain to be,
But it is the thoughts that remain for you,
And we all wait for the answers.

I know you, like your family
And miss you the same,
Wherever you are,
Lighter than air,
Stronger than the wind,
I visit your place. I feel the love,

I think of you on days of birth,
And still, have laughter and pride of many things we had accomplished,
But still, I roam without you,
We had so much more to do,

I don't mean to be selfish,
But I guess I am still in shock,
You were my only true friend,

I was told; we are lucky if we can say we have at least one (a true friend)
I know you were that one,
You know you were also,
So as a friend, to another I ask;
Give us all strength, at our hardest points.
And be with us all in our prayers.

Love Forever As Your Friend.

Success

To some success is a family,

To some success is money,

But to the other percentage of people in the world success is waking up each day.

Waking up, seeing the sun and smiling.

Feeling the warmth of the sun on your face,

Closing your eyes and digesting the creativity of life.

Now, with that as a thought, you should think which percentage you are?

The Dream Of Life

When he woke up, he heard a voice that called to him,
It was a childlike voice, which could be heard slowly and distractingly,
He received a chill from standing on the outside of the bed,
And looking around he thought he was dreaming,
Everything seemed to be the opposite of reality.
He went on and used every sense to get out alive,
He tried to go towards the child's voice,
He tried
She kept calling over and over again; he would walk towards the cry,
Just to hear the voice coming from a different location.

A dream in his mind, but also it was a sign,
A sign, which told him to be careful from the voices in the darkness,
The voices he couldn't see.

Maybe they were there, waiting, looking, staring, but his mind didn't
allow the physical Shape,

The physical image.

The closer he would seem, the further his mind was, away from the
truth,
which was in his face always.

He realized this!
He returned in his starting position from looking and closed his eyes,
He remembered his heart. He remembered his reasoning,

He heard the cry for help again.

The child's cry, which gave him an even greater chill this time,
He was ready though, ready to meet up with the destiny that God
wanted him to see,

He crept forward to the sound,
As he grew closer this time he waited, the sound grew louder and this
time did not leave. He opened the door.

There he saw a light, a light that was bright blue and drifted in circles
in the shadows to show a faint object in a tornado-like cloud.

He began to cry,
He realized he had seen his life too much now and that finally this was
his end.

He walked near the light, which scared but fascinated him immensely.

He wondered if it was real, it felt like a dream.

The closer he paced near; he felt a great presence of love and emotion,
But not from himself from the room like he was surrounded by beings
in the shadows. he closed his eyes once again and took another step.
He wanted to scream, he even tried but his voice was collapsed, maybe
it was a dream?

He opened his eyes and started to see visions of the blue light circling around the room, they were made out as human-like creatures, but it was clearly something he had never seen before, so he concentrated, he made out their appearances to be human,

They reached out their hands and pointed to the greater light in the center of the room; he collapsed to his knees. He couldn't speak, and now a powerful force stunned his body, but his mind was reacting in ways he couldn't understand, but still, he knew he was in control.

He smiled,

Then appeared, just a child's face from the tornado-like force
A powerful child it seemed to him, and also from what he could read with his mind from the others perched in a circle around them both.

The face came nearer to him, but he couldn't move, he didn't want to He felt no danger, only love, the face grew nearer and kissed his forehead, smiling.

He smiled back, and from the blue lighted shadows a hand appeared pointing him towards the greater light down a pathway or tunnel which appeared as the hand did,

He was mesmerized by such magic and started to gain feeling again in his body; he started to stand, as did the beings around him,

They started to become more lifelike as he fully arose.

He smiled again and felt a great wind, which only he could feel,
The wind let him understand this happening, he was dying,
But still, so young.
So full of life,

The child's face still pointing towards the tunnel was the invitation.

But with his mind he reached out to the child, and embraced him, he knelt down again and slowly expressed he was not ready. Then he apologized.

The child's face slowly looked back towards the tunnel looked back at him and granted him his peace. Peace to remain with life. To remain and live, and for the first time in his life, he knew what it meant.

The child again kissed his forehead and disappeared.

The man closed his eyes once again as tears streamed his face, he was ready to live again, having experienced something so amazing, he was on his way to life, again.

When he opened his eyes, the room was silent, and he slowly walked near his bed where it all started, which felt like a dream, he entered his room to see his body laying comfortably on his bed, it startled him, but he again smiled, closed his eyes and was ready for a new day,

His last thought that night was (when will I ever get such a visit again?)

He was now ready to live. Some never get a second chance, but he was pure, maybe one of the purest the child has ever seen. He was granted fidelity to live a new life, a new life, which would make everything seem (to the soul) merely a dream,

But trust me, it can be a reality.

The Ocean Of Your Soul

The one place for me to see,
Life at its fullest,
Is the ocean, the water so blue?

My eyes cry from memories by the sea,
It's also the one place which has brought you closer.

Life is a battle; it has been for us both,
But together, we can learn from our friend the ocean.

It has power, it helps us live, and it flows throughout us all,
But he is our friend because when we are near, we learn a lesson,

Smell, this beautiful smell can clear us of our past.

Touch, a great feeling of rebirth, to be cleansed for a new future.

Taste, like the feeling of a first kiss, salty and warm, but always bringing
sensations uncontrollable.

Sight, the amazing visualizations of water, seeing the force of the wind
on the waves and how it somehow can show you caution in life is a
virtue. You can also see its ever-changing color.

This may be the changing of moods for the ocean, just like in human
life. From green to blue, too far underneath black, and sometimes, if

you try hard enough, you can see the whole light spectrum prism itself, when the sun appears and fades.

This is life. Beautiful Life.

A life many never see when they look at something so common as the ocean.

But life begins with water, and it is also a part of your body. So take another look and smile,
Maybe even say thank you in your mind. Because you have just met once again your reason for survival.

If you listen closely, you may hear your reason for life; you may even hear your reason to live.

But, No matter what reason you think or see from such beauty. Always remember this,

You are unique, and presently you are living, (reading). Tomorrow happened, today is happening,

But tomorrow can always change your life!

If you have trouble, stress, doubt, or pain. If you see these words to be true? Wherever you are, just close your eyes, and remember a day by the ocean.
You will be healed.

The Past of Your Youth

My past is a wild one,
But it's mine,
My life is a challenge,
But I am doing fine,
Finer than I have been,
Finer than I will be

Today is a new day
Brighter than yesterday
Finer than the sun, hotter than it's warmth,
Easier than tomorrow.
Smiling as it sets.

Crying while I sleep
Thinking where I should be
Can't fall to dream,
Just falling deep in thought
Until my decision is made,
To change,
Then when I awake
I will be alive

Remembering when I was a child
On Christmas day,
To see the tree, to see the lights,
To remember the colors,
And to want to play,

To run outside and feel the cold,
To jump into the wind and feel life.

That's where I am, serious
Happy; remembering happiness.
To see simply that your life can always be what you want,
As long as you see,
The warmth of the wind; when your life was young

Together - Always

Struggle, the pain of families, joy, then struggle.
Worry,
What can it bring?
Growing up quickly in just a month,
Seriousness, getting it all together,
In just a month,

Laziness at the first of the year,
To seriousness of a man and woman, who are confused in love?
Confused but fused together in destiny.

Love,

That's where it will come from,
Growing old together and maybe enjoying life for a change,
New life can only be brought from God.

A god who has a destiny for us all,
Making us drill our minds for the success of what he will bring us as
a career.

Then the stress,
The stress of the drilling of the mind to take chances,
Because I simply took a chance on love, and it worked.

Forever, hopefully
Success, hopefully
Trust, hopefully

Together, always!

Understanding Love

Take it slow,
How could it ever be words by someone who knows what they want?

When you know what you want, you examine the issue,
You think,
Then you, for a moment become someone else,
You think about the moment,
Why, the situation,
But if you visualize something, and know you want it,
There will never be anything to stand in your way, of your goal.

Your goal? Being the object,
The thing.

You sacrifice; you settle your thoughts,
Then you think of an outcome,
When it comes to you, you act on it,
You walk in, you receive.

But truly to me, in a heart that has been there,
I know love,
Love that could be, love that may be,
But never to have doubts or regrets,
I want love, but it is not that simple, it's not supposed to be.

Take it slow, should never be, but it is the situation,
Only knowing what you want can be your problem,
Especially when you want the one thing you can't seem to understand.

Love, I wish it were that easy.

Watch What You Wash Away

I'm not the man you think of,
I'm not a man at all
I am the wind,
Dust.

I run with the air
And have seen murder,
So it would no longer be a good thing,
To see each other further.

Do you understand?
Or should I explain more,
You cleaned, I showed up.
You looked down,
I was there, then as you turned around
I was in your hair,

You washed me out,
It was easy to leave,
But when I go, I know you will grieve.

You don't want me
Explanations are easy,
Goodbyes are hell,
You looked too hard when you saw me on the ground,
So you must leave as well.
Do not cry, I never spoke.

I just looked,
And love, I could never,
So let me stay, alone, bringing sickness
Witnessing all,
Through travel of air.
Plainly dust.

Next time leave me there?

Awake In Time

We are all just a wake in time.
Searching for meaning as the years drift on.
We feel, love, care, raise, and teach.
We question, feel, run, and reach.

We may all be looking for a wake in times that have drifted.
Better years of memories that remind us of smiles and fevers that brought blankets of unconditional support and love.
The warmth allowed you to feel.
The feelings are there to remind us that times existence will not always be here.
The frequencies melt into faded spirals onto the earth they were created.

Can we just get to later years with our free will intact?
Do we have a choice that we continue the years even after we choose to be on vacation of the minds we carry?

In sickness and in health
No success or plenty of wealth
The outcomes are only up to the continued frequencies we created.
The loves we felt.

Our choices can bring us existence or end us immediately.

And so we continue awake in time.

When I Focus - Always

When I Focus I could do anything,
But when I think, too hard, my thoughts wander.

Wondering about love, will it be?
Or will it fade, not on my part!
But it takes two to be in love,
And yet it leaves me speechlessly drifting.

What may come of the future of two?
Laughter, compassion, smiles of joy.
Or hurt, addiction, loss, all while (no matter what)
Constantly there for each other.

Love, an emotion I have felt, but never so strongly as I feel now.

And even now, strongly thinking of the only one I want,
Staring at pictures of laughter, I cannot always be there physically.
Not my fault I know, but I still trust.

Soon, I will return with flowers from my soul,
Will there be more trust or hurt,
In a perfect world, I would pray for trust,
But this is no perfect world.

My love is deep, strong, loyal, honest, and forever,
It will just take (time) to see and know,
Just how much she will always mean to me!

Then she will be proud to see,
What her life has given to a person such as I.

With time, I know in my heart, we will be together always!

Chapter 2

MOTIVATION

Motivation is everything to me. It is one of my favorite words. I do not remember a time that I have not or did not want to be motivated. I think staying motivated is what keeps us wanting to experience everything we have not seen in this life already. I also think that it's what keeps us learning and makes us want to learn more. I think having a drive for life is part of what makes us flip a switch and activate our D.N.A. It shows us truly what we are made of and makes us strive for new goals.

There were times when we feel restricted in this body from sickness that we feel we can't go further, but that is when it is very important to focus within and view ourselves as the amazing energies we all are. When we visualize our paths, there is no way we will stay restricted.

~ Kevin J. Ste Marie

Finding Strength From Past Love

Falling out of love is hard,
But falling back is even harder,
Trying to figure out exactly what is important,
And trying to be strong at the same time,
It's not possible,
Always an obstacle,
That's life I guess,
But GOD has something for us to do,
Maybe it's being single? Married
For some reason, you know it will work out,
Are you tired of asking permission to love?
You just want to, do just that, LOVE.
I cant. I am slapped each day while still looking,
Waiting for it to stumble, in my lap.
Hard or soft, please just stumble, I need it.
I'm not lonely,
I just want to love someone,
I'm scared. But I need to survive.

LOVE, I have no regrets, but my life has been circled around the word.
Imagine your whole life circled around a word?
That is where I have found my strength.

Friends of the Night

There is so much to live for
The people you may meet the next day, the people you met the day
before to remember and say hello again when the time comes
There is also time to say hello to you
To feel your mind in a certain place, only you can enter, and leave with
a feeling of hope

A feeling that you will fight to survive with every breath that the
world gives you to breathe. However, sometimes in life, we may feel
depression, anger, fright, and pain
These are feelings I know well. Nevertheless, to all this negativity, you
must find the center of yourself, that fire that burns so deep that it gives
you the strength to open your eyes each morning.
Your first thought, usually your best. Like your first kiss, of course,
fright, the feeling of uncontrollable love will come from your fire telling
you this kiss you can never take back
You will never have another

For some, anger; to never feel firsts such as these
I drop an hour of my life for these people for the strength to know they
can live on and survive
Depression, I have been here so many times, It has brought me the most
strength in my life
The greatest ideas and difficulties to accomplish
However, what is important is that I, and I alone conquered my battles.
Also, that I can look back on my best days living, knowing I am loved.
Knowing that I have people who care for me.

Even when I sometimes do not want to be cared for

Is it something about me? Maybe

But to my happiness in life, I would give it up to see others who are less
fortunate feel how good it is to love themselves
Finally when your fire is found, when the courage has entered the mind
can you look off a mountain and breathe in the air knowing what it
must feel like to be free. Free like me!

This is from the deepest pains and smiles of my heart. I hope you too,
One day can feel what I do

This is my wish for you.

Just A Thought

Everything in my life came rushing back,
Rushing back like a child running from fear,
Creating a new person,
Creating the old me
Money, success, happiness,
Without a friend in the world.

My old life?
No, my new one, just a little altered.
Thank you, GOD.
I know I will get what I am looking for.
I am not alone.

Lasting Impression

I didn't want to kiss you, but I had to see
The love that was meant for me,
Even though you couldn't understand,
That love that was meant,

I understand, but what am I to do?
You kissed me you had to have loved what you felt
You kissed me back and showed emotion,
You let your lips run through me like a train in free-flowing movement,
Run through my heart as I felt you, felt your soul.
Softly and slowly,
All night
But, what counts is that I'm here
Holding you
How long can it last?

Life Is Short - Wisdom

Tonight is a night for dreaming,
A night so perplex with the evidence of self-assurance,
Tonight I dream,
Dream of a better place
A place of hunger a place of despair,
A place in which I was born,
The earth, A ball of light,
Submersed into an atmosphere of moving tranquility,
I read I learn, but still, I will die, as you have,
Dead in a coffin,
I will rot,
Rot like a fish on the deck,
A baby bird in the nest,
Rotting used; for another to come,
And take me away for dinner
Can I stop it no?
That is life,
But I can make a change,
A change for the better,
A change for the future,

Can I do it?

Maybe,

But I will have to believe,
Believe in my hurt,

Believe in my pain,
Also believe that after I am different, I will never be the same,
But then,
And only then
Will I,
And I alone be able to gasp in the air like a champion,
Alone for me to breathe,
The last breath.

And when I am finished
I will become the thinnest of air.

The air, which moves me,
The air, which is life
The air, which makes it.

But not forever.

Love and Influence

In many years, I have watched people fall,
Fall from influence.

It's even harder to watch such a thing when it's someone you love.
Unconditionally.
It's hard to sit there and wait,
As the hours go by,
You want to cry,
But your strength guides you,
And this is when you survive,

Then you decide for yourself whether or not it's worth boggling your mind over.

But still, you are boggled.

And realistically you are influenced.

Influenced by your love.

Love,

It could be my only influence.

Maybe one day Ill understand,

At the touch of God's hand,

Will I find the answers I seek?

But until I receive, I remain to be challenged.

A candle will light,

It will burn all night,

The wax will melt,

The same as a human heart bleeds,

But this is our reminder,

As big as a heart could be,

It still dies in the end.

We are left to fly with the wind.

Just dust in the wind.

Story of Love and Waiting

I was just getting over a break-up, ok, it had been about a year since the breakup, but I guess I was full of doubt and regret. I just didn't get myself anymore, I hoped to find it a month ago, but I figured I would die trying.

The next day was an afternoon get together at my grandmother's house. My grandmother is the type of woman who enjoys taking care of people, much like myself (at times) but on this day I was feeling down, like always I just couldn't get social. I mean I smile I dance, I even laugh but inside I'm just not the same.

I looked up and my vision blurred from the sun. Then I stood up looked around and walked around the house; I started to look at all of the people who had just finished their Sunday meal full and enjoying the air outside by the trees.

There was a chill in my body at a sudden glance, and I was nervous from the site of a girl I once knew intimately but never had a relationship with. She was beautiful, I had always thought so, since the first time I had ever seen her. I never get intimidated to talk, but for the first time, I was there. Was this Love? I couldn't move, and my feelings of aggravation had swallowed me whole. They were suddenly gone.

Her green eyes were still there more beautiful as I have ever seen them, her face still as soft as I had ever seen leaning up against the house outside with the sun warming her face. I was so intimidated but knew in my mind I had to get close.

As I approached her, she recognized me and then softly smiled I asked her if I could sit. She softly looked at her mother as she smiled and said sure, slightly stood and greeted me with a hug. I couldn't believe how her beauty remained with her through the years that had passed. I wanted to kiss her. I saw her lips so soft and wet as she ran her tongue over a wine glass she was drinking from.

As her mother started to make her way into other conversations, we started to talk as if there was no past at all, like we had picked up from there and started the very next day.

It was enlightening to see her, and even more enlightening to not be rejected. I couldn't understand this feeling. Beauty. And it was the feeling of love that I had felt that had smothered me once again. I couldn't move but talked to her like we were already married. As close as an older couple enjoying retirement for the first day.

She grabbed the back of my head and smiled slightly drunk. I could tell she remembered when we kissed the first time. As I looked into her eyes, I couldn't speak and fell into her arms, to receive a soft hug. As I put my arms around her I fell for her immediately all over again. Did she feel the same? She leaned forward and kissed my neck softly. Such a kiss scared me, but I wanted to be scared. I enjoyed the feeling.

I leaned forward once again and looked into her glistening green eyes. I kissed her again. Five times better than the first and she obliged me with the rest kissing me back just as softly as she also did the first time. I could feel her hands she wanted it.

And I just hoped that it wouldn't end. I had often prayed for this feeling I didn't want it to end. So when it did, I cringed; she smiled and told me she also prayed to take it easy because there would be no regrets this time. I smiled almost with tears in my eyes. Full of love, I wanted to scream. I loved her. I knew I did. She was amazing.

Now all I have to do is find her.

The Consumer

Everyone walks the earth,
And ever since birth we were taught that escape was wrong,
Escape,

Escape from normal life is wrong,
But who ever listens,

Even I am guilty,
I am proud of my guilt though,
I have learned from it,

Even now I enjoy one of life's great addictions,
And even still, I am no addict.

I just enjoy the escape,
The escape which is away from the norm, away from serious.

It teaches me we will not live forever,
We are not supposed to,

I am no psychic,
But I can swear, telepathy has touched me.

My creative mind is what I am; It was God's gift to me.
As was my life,

He will take them both when he is ready,
Whenever he is ready, I will be ready for the new mission.

The mission of the new life, the new world, which no human has seen,
but has been very Close to, in their dreams.
I will be ready to meet my new, and old friends.

Create me a mind I will bring you flowers of my heart,
Show me the water, and I will swim in your soul.

Shower me with life.
Let my dreams fly to the sea, spill my ashes upon your breath.

I want the world to breathe me in, but not as entertainment.
Just as a dreamer, a believer, a lover of all.

Love me, love all, that is why we are here,
Be creative,
Live your life, because when you become a statue in your tomb,
It will be too late.

Don't waste it. Take your addictions and make them. Refuse to let them
make you.

You are the consumer!

The Entrance and the Exit

We are all just a wake in time.
Searching for meaning as the years drift on.
We feel, love, care, raise, and teach.
We question, feel, run, and reach.

We may all be looking for a wake in times that have drifted.
Better years of memories that remind us of smiles and fevers that
brought blankets of unconditional support and love.
The warmth allowed you to feel.
The feelings are there to remind us that times existence will not always
be here.
The frequencies melt into faded spirals onto the earth they were created.

Can we get to later years with our free will intact?
Do we have a choice that we continue the years even after we choose to
be on vacation of the minds we carry?

In sickness and in health
No success or plenty of wealth
The outcomes are only up to the continued frequencies we created.
The loves we felt.

Our choices can bring us existence or end us immediately.

And so we continue awake in time.

Throw Me Away - Let Me Find My Balance

Run me out of the house,

Scream, yell, push, shove, me; please,

Let me focus on a new day, homelessness, pain, despair; it can only lead to honor,

But only if I remain focused and speak.

Speak to the only, which is I,

No hesitation, just scream my voice, sing, dance, experience, just life.

Keep my head up, running gently then fast, until I collapse,

Keep my arms free until I have a relapse, of everything,

Everything spoke above,

I want to live, and to live fully; it will keep me balanced.

I want the world to feel my heart.

Then I can examine, examine a full clean experience when people come together and show love,

Not just for money, but for unconditional, balance,

The criminal, friends with businessman

Father to son, mother to daughter,

Uncontrollably flowing until the end.

Time Is Short - Don't Be Cruel

I am hurt.
I want to be
I need to be,

Because the more I push
The more I gain
The more I am shoved

The more I continue to be a machine
A machine, with the ideas and mentality to kill anyone,
Not with force
But by the mind

My gun in your mouth,
Your knife in my back,
Stabbed again,
By the people you trust

Whos next?
Bring them on,
I will only grow mentally and with time,
I will learn to overpower your soul

Then you will know you were wrong,
Wrong mentally, physically,
For thinking that once in your life, it was right to be deceitful
To the one person,

The person who would have saved you
Saved your life from anything wrong

The day will come,
Soon, as time flies by
I will not go away
Persistence has become my only friend

And once time is gained,
You will be fooled,
As I was in the beginning.
Nevertheless, that will be the end.
Forever!

Until Death Do I Part

I dreamed last night of a new life,
A life of a smile,

It lasted for just a little while.
But when I awoke, I was left to think,
My eyes were wide; I didn't blink,

Faller I sink,
I cry,
I try to believe,
I try,
But nothing is there,
We will see,

Or maybe someone else,
I am alone for now,
By myself,

Alone to think,
Alone to analyze,
Alone,
To write
To think some more,
To fall in my head until I die.

Wondering For Love

Sometimes, I hear you,

At times I never know you are there.

At times, I love you,

But At times, I know you don't.

At times I procrastinate to find you,

And at times I hear your voice, in my mind, and run to the phone.

I know I am searching, but at

Times, wonder if I should be, should I be?

The feeling makes my procrastination fall; it makes my mind spin,

It makes me return to happiness,

It makes me understand why we live,

And helps me to understand why we die.

I can live for your beauty

What is stopping me?

Is it that I am wrong for you or, is it,

Is it I.

Stubborn.

Do you need me as I need you?

Are you dreaming about me?

Like I am you?

Are you scared and intimidated to call also?

I would be a fool not to try to miss out on the love that could be mine

And yours.

I hope maybe I find you, your #, your new #,

Your new location?

Where are you?

Let's start our life

You know what's weird you even make me smile
And I don't even know you; don't even know your face.
But I have an idea.
And I would love to get started, so bump into me,
I am waiting!

Chapter 3

SEARCHING

When you close your eyes what is it that you see? I see tomorrow. Even though you may not be able to change who you are today, you can change the thoughts. Your thoughts are your doorway to tomorrow's physical happiness. It is also the doorway to the opposite if you do not learn to control these thoughts. We are born and for some we are not as perfect as some may believe. For some it takes time to cleanse and it's how a curse can turn into a blessing to have to be able to this at such a young age. For myself I forgive the way I entered this world for making me always be reminded that I started early. I considered it a true blessing to start searching. I am thankful that I never stopped. Even beyond this world I will always be learning and searching. But no matter how much I search I know that the future of everything I have ever learned started with forgiveness and love.

~ Kevin J. Ste Marie

By Your Side - Wishing

I want to die by your side,
I wouldn't bear any other pain,
Of being without,
Of never being able to see you,
Let me hug,
Let me hold you, one last time, to seal it with a kiss,
Make love in your arms just knowing it will end.
Together, as we were meant to be.
This thought would be heaven.

Destiny Awaits Us

One person will walk down a road,
Not knowing that when he turns around his past turns into dust under his feet.
Looking back on the past, and the roads you have walked down have been mere old roads of embarrassment, old love, and silence.
Then the wind blows, you turn around and remember what you were doing, forgetting the past again.

You should remember that your past is who you are,
Never forgetting your old loves, your old embarrassments and the never-ending silence of wanting; to release the growth of whom you once were as a person.

You were sick once, and when you awoke, there they were, the people who loved you, the people who you smiled at, even though your sickness drained you.
Because you knew you were loved.

Another time you were scared and had no one to turn to...alone.
You dealt with those problems yourself and were proud of the outcome.
Pleased to know that the next day,
There were no problems at all. Just dust, under your feet.

We all will awake one day, but many will not be healed to know that we are creators of our destiny.

Our destiny awaits us.

For Someone Still Waiting

I never thought in my life I could ever be so complete,
Until I met one,
I close my eyes and see your face, and then I smile,
Because I know I have never been so happy,
I could not possibly wipe off the smile, ever.
You have brought me life, the other side of heaven I could have only
read about,
I am thankful.

We make love.
Your touch makes me silent, warm, never scared,
Your kiss makes me melt, as I think even in such little time we have
shared,
Your heart is full of compassion, full of life.
I can only wait for the day, proving my love with you as my wife,
You will always bring me joy,
With your smiles of love and laughter,
Soul mates forever and ever after.
Connected as one sharing love like it was our first time,
My arms around you, kissing, sharing, and joining love,
I thank GOD above.
I thank your parents for making such beauty,
I kiss your neck, then your back as I slowly rub every inch of you,
You are amazing,
Your lips are incredibly soft,
I can't let go.

All I can think is how much I want you to feel every part of me that is love for you.

The older you get, the more my love will grow,
Don't be scared, and only love will show,
If you need me close your eyes, I will always bring you strength,
I will always be patient and kind,
A love like ours is hard to find!

Please know this,
I am here for you, in just the time I have known you have brought my life meaning.
This will only grow.
Don't change a thing.

You are my angel, fly with me in your dreams.

I Search Who Will I Find

Have you ever wondered what could be right in your hands?
I did until I stumbled into the hands of someone so amazing,
All my life,
I have met people,
And now I know they were just a test,
A test to get me ready for what I finally found,
I have never seen anything so clear.

I have never felt anything so real,
Every moment together,
Every kiss, every conversation.

Perfect,

I used to think nothing in this world was perfect; I used to think life
had no meaning at times,
Now I see, clearly, just how right it can be, just how perfect it should be,

Conversations of life,
Kissing like it was the last time,
Could only forever bring happiness?

Happiness for us.

And now I miss you

I miss you so much because I look at the memory of where we were earlier,

And want it to be.

I will fall asleep, but I will fantasize about you, no one else,

I know now no one else could make me smile like this,

When I close my eyes I know, I will dream about you,

In my dream, I will hold a smile,

A smile for you.

And when we look at each other we will kiss,

Like we do every time,

Like we will see in the future,

I will be patient to hold you.

But I will be dreaming of the reality each day.

I have waited a lifetime, for happiness, I finally found it.

I found you.

Mirror of Life

When you take a minute and look at yourself in the mirror,
you can see what you want to be.

It may hurt, but look deeper inside yourself.
You will find the opening of your soul's existence.
Even if you are a dreamer, your dreams will make you,
Dream, because if there were no room for the dream, your brain would
release it.
The mind body and soul want you to be happy; they want you to smile,
frown, and cry,
But in our world which is filled with despair, only we are standing in
the way of our true purpose, only we are in that mirror looking.

The purpose that many will find will be a (comfortable) one,
But to the other people, who are trendsetters in life, to them, comfortable
was just not good enough,
I write these words in my heart and believe their meanings to be a
religion

The religion that is I, the religion that makes me unique, makes me
(whole)

And deeply, love.

Which has escaped me, escaped me like a thief, waiting patiently for his
next to steal. Beware of this soul; his mind is vicious.

So apparently, when we mold our conversations in the mirror of life,
We might be as evident that this person that we see looking back is cloning your thoughts individually.

Reading our minds, to guide us,
This can truly be GOD.

God: which is why we stare, at that mirror and one day make a change,
Change? That is why the mirror exists. Look at it tonight, and before you brush,
Think.

Because one look can change your life...

No Address - No Number

Tonight, I search for a friend
A search well said,
I look at papers with numbers,
I search for an address.

I wander in my car,
I do not attempt to stop,
Just drive, searching;
Still not yet to find,
I drive to a place,
My place of hope,

I walk down the dark halls,
I climb the flights of stairs,
Very dark, yet pure, I keep climbing,
I reach the top, the stories high.

I feel the wind as I reach the edge,
It speaks to me softly, as if I was flying.
I lean against the ropes, of my abandoned place,
My abandoned building
I look down. I am fully surrounded.
I can easily jump, but why?

To end a life not lived yet,
To never see if I can make what I want to become?
Or maybe I come here for a sign,
Who knows, I'll find out one day?
But for now, I am drawn here, to my place,
Abandoned, to the world, but not erased,
We have a lot in common it seems
We are friends,

One day I will be there,
As will my friend. And it is there I will sit, once again.
Loved as a visitor, and still searching.
I cannot live like my friend though,
He is becoming something, although a building, his hallways I listen,
He tells me his stories, what he has been through,
I listen without prejudice.
We are so different,
But he will give me a degree,
He cries now, but soon he will smile with paint, art, and modern furniture.
But as friends, I will truly see the inner him, his true light,
Unconditionally.

Every time I visit we will cry,
Every time I am near, he will know,
He wants good things for me, and no matter what happens he will also know the real me,
Inside.

I am leaving him soon. He can feel it.

I found my sign; He has helped me more than he will ever know,

No address, no number, but we will always have what's most important,

Our memories.

Poem For Faith

When you look at me,
You wonder if I can bring you hurt
When I see you
I know I could never
When you touch me
You burn inside
When I felt you near
I wanted to cry

I will never meet anyone like you again,
I know this in my heart
You bring me happiness,
You bring me, love,
Every time, unconditionally.

It feels amazing to be wanted,
To be trusted; to be seen as you do me,
And thinking back on love, from the past,
I clearly know I was never in love like this,
Everything is in love, emotion, physical stimulation, and my senses,
Alive - for you, the future with you, and the understanding we will
bring to each other.

Every night I will pray,
Every night I will think,
But every day,

I will know I have found what it was I have been praying for since I
was born,
You bring me life; you make it real.
And I want to show you how I feel.
So every time, you look at me
Anytime you need me, just call my name,
And I will bring you hope.

Sometimes People Think

Sometimes I close my eyes and wonder,
If maybe there's a form of meditation for falling in love,
A meditation so strong that your mind and soul are fused together in
a realm,
A realm of unconsciousness,
A dream,
To simply fall in love is the hardest thing to figure out,
But when it stumbles upon you, you are embodied.
You lose your train of thought, some people anyway,
I analyze it, that's why I am alone currently because I am looking for
the force,
The realm,

The realms, which while you are sleeping make you, wake up and want
to do anything just to get a glance and just that (who you love).

Many are in love, they will remain to be, but the old ways are just not
taught anymore,
When someone speaks to another about finding each other, it is
considered (weird) or maybe even (crazy).

I know the older ways expression, unity, loyalty, respect, and love
making so strong that every touch is like the first time, does that make
me different,
I hope so because I am not changing.

But my analytic mind has taught me to keep it to myself, until the right moment. If I would have done this a long time ago I may already be married.

But I also know my soul mate to be will be able to look me in the face and know I love her just with a glance, we will be able to know that every time we kiss it will be emotional not just to kiss, and will also know that when I make love to her my mind will be under the impression that it may be the last time ever.

I want this, and I also know there is a woman who wants the same.
Until then I wait and focus on my meditation,
The meditation of dreaming into my soul's realm, for the person who will set my soul on fire.

When she is found,

no wind, no water, and no powerful force will ever set apart the love we will have.

The Child Taught Me Life

I walk to the river and witness a horrible thing,

A woman kills her son,

Did she want a daughter? Did she hate the pain of birth?

I couldn't relate, I could only just sit there and wait,

I waited; to be noticed, waited to heal the woman, to show her that her thoughts could have been avoided,

So I made a sound,

She turned up and looked in my eyes,

I know what she felt

She felt the fire. Fire running through her veins from my compassion, and purity,

I made her see what she did was wrong,

And as we both stared and read each other's thoughts fragrantly,

We then watched her beautiful baby sons soul rise to heaven.

I smiled at such beauty.

As my smile grew, I then watched the woman's soul start to feel pain,

And nervousness,

She wanted to take back what she had done,

She wanted, but she also wanted to be taken in and held, just like her son,

She didn't know how, I saw it clearly, and her only motivation was hurt.

I then made a serious face, kept calm, and watched the woman drop dead into the river,

I felt her pain as she died, now she has no pain, no son,

But I have the memory, of watching them lying together in the river, bodies cold, and holding hands,

I saw no spirit of the woman's body, as I saw in the child. But I knew this,

She (still) had work to do; her soul's accomplishments were not over.

As she killed her son, she had also killed many others, herself: mentally.

She will return home after she has made what she did a mental picture no more.

I waited for an hour, until the bodies had vanished into the moonlight down the river.

Still holding hands.

What did this mean?

That I am intuitive? That I was screwed for witnessing? Maybe, but to me, as I walked home, after being a witness to something so hainess, I also knew I viewed a rebirth of a beautiful baby boy's soul.

You only witness situations that startle you when you want to be startled, and I wasn't, so I guess maybe it left me to remember every time I should have loved, I should have hugged, I should have showed emotion. As my walk home drew on, I was haunted by my horrible thoughts of life and was sorry for them immensely. I hugged my soul with my mind and began to cry from emotion. Then I felt the warmth like no other. Amazing warmth, like feeling the warm sun as it rises on the beach. Slowly burning your face.

I cried even harder, I thought death was near, but I remained, so after I felt the warmth, I smiled. Into Healed of my hurt from life, Free to live a new one.

There is no doubt in my mind that I should have died walking home that night.

The feeling of pain I felt walking in the dirt stunned me to my feet. My chest burned, and my tears were like cinder streaming down my face. And then a force turned cold inside of me as if all my pain was released through my fire-like, then turning to ice as if to give me a fever. I grew sick mentally from no remorse; I just wanted to let the woman see she was wrong with my eyes. But before The act, sitting there, I asked for a sign. A sign to show me there can be a better life to lead. A sign of hope, I wanted to repent.

I thank the sun, every day, for whatever reason, for such a gift, for being there. Its presence helped me realize I was not the only witness.

Now, seven years since that occurrence: I write,
I write about the change I was given. Because maybe you will never witness such an act, but by reading it, you can understand my thoughts and realize what I was forced to do.
When I die, I know now my soul will be as free as the child's,

I will hover, just as his soul did, and will be there to meet him.
I will reach out with a hug and tell, thank you.

Thank you all.

The Love Which Kills Many

He sat down for another lesson,
Lessons that he would never forget but would never live to regret.
He sat trembling, to the point that he had to get away from his fears

The fears that he was running from,
No result to drugs, no result to anything negative, and no turning to
religion.
If the religion were helping it would be inside of him,
So he waits no longer he climbs to the very place.
The place where he first opened his eyes and visualized.

The building

The first thing visualized when he first stepped foot to try and start a
new life for himself
It would be the one place he would then end it all.

That which is so hard to do had seen very clearer now,
Just jump,
That is all. To leap into the air like the baby bird that will fly or die.
I would do one of the two also, although one was a lot more likely

Then the pain would stop
Stop the hurt
Stop the famine in my heart, forever

Streaks of blood trickle, from my eyes, tears of the desire of not wanting
to die to give the redness of blood, a salty warm taste.
What will I look like dead?
What will they say then?
Will they even cry?
Maybe but it will last only for a week, a month, a year,
Maybe on its anniversary will I be thought of.

For taking my life
Hurting my family
And hurting the people who love me,
Nevertheless, although they will hurt, I will be in heaven, because No
one should hurt like this,

No one should cry to gain strength
And, no one should run their mind non stop into the wall, to simply cry
in the end, from more hurt, like you are addicted to the pain,

Like a victim

The fall will be beautiful, but the landing will be even better
The pain, although the worst kind,
Will peel my skin and burn me like fire.
My bones would break, and my heart would stop

However, even still in my death, I know I could never forget love.

The love that killed me.

The Sun - Can It Heal

I burn in the sun,
But somehow it heals my depression,
Heals my soul,
The bugs, they bite me,
But still, it's a bite I bear.

I don't mind the pain,
It keeps me from going insane.

I drift with my eyes closed
A lazy sunbather,
And wander into my mind,
Into the suns warmth,
I try to feel, its fire,
I try to feel the singe,

I feel the energy,
It flows through my body,
It brings me strength.

I swat away a bug and kill it,
Now there's one less to worry about,
Much like my problems,

If only it were that easy.

Tomorrow Is Our Fate

I'm easy to please,
Just show me, love.
I have shown you mine,
Would it be hard, to even try?

A heart can only break so many times,
How many has yours been broken?
Is it that your mind is not complete?
Did you wish me another day?

I guess I can't help that.
But I did fall in love along the way,
And inside, my happiness for you still grows,
Even though I think at times, your soul drifts from me,
Under the influence, maybe,
But love never fades, unless it is hurt,
Pain, instead of smiles,
Smiles to try and ease it.

When crying starts, you are there,
And when held by the only one,
You are safe; feel safe even without anyone,
For you, for anything!

My arms are stretched, raised to show you, love,
Don't laugh,
You have shown me affection, understanding, and compassion,
But I wonder, what can tomorrow bring?

Printed in the United States
by Baker & Taylor Publisher Services